T0194694

Whispers of Miracles

YEGANEH KARIMI

WESTBOW
PRESS®
A DIVISION OF THOMAS NELSON
& ZONDERVAN

This book is a work of non-fiction. Unless otherwise noted, the author and the publisher make no explicit guarantees as to the accuracy of the information contained in this book and in some cases, names of people and places have been altered to protect their privacy.

WestBow Press books may be ordered through booksellers or by contacting:

WestBow Press
A Division of Thomas Nelson & Zondervan
1663 Liberty Drive
Bloomington, IN 47403
www.westbowpress.com
844-714-3454

ISBN: 978-1-6642-1856-7 (sc)
ISBN: 978-1-6642-1857-4 (hc)
ISBN: 978-1-6642-1855-0 (e)

Library of Congress Control Number: 2021900188

Print information available on the last page.

WestBow Press rev. date: 03/22/2021

To one of my dearest friends, Miss Hamideh Yassai, and my family, Koohyar, Sara, and Koohzad Karimi.

This book would not have been possible without their support and the amazing care that I received.

Coronavirus

AS OF THIS WRITING, IT has been a month since we first learned the horrible news, from all over the world, about a new virus, COVID-19. Many people ignored the warning about this virus, thinking that different countries probably would control it very soon.

However, we were wrong; this virus is still at the forefront of the news. The entire world is shocked because the virus can spread to people very quickly. Most countries have started to quarantine the people in order to prevent emergency situations.

Everything in this world has a contradiction—a bright side and a dark side. Therefore, if we look at the bright side of COVID-19, we can realize that people who are in quarantine, perhaps staying at home with most of the members of the family, are able to communicate with one another. The value systems in the family are nurtured with respect to family cultures and foundations.

Self-care and self-discipline can affect daily schedules. The world may return to the peace-and-quiet place. There is nothing now to make people interact—everything is closed, even schools, colleges, and educational centers. People hope to return to work.

It is interesting, as it seems that God is helping us to appreciate what we had before. Life is beautiful, and the power of gratitude can open our eyes to observe that life is not about us.

It could be beyond the universe, but Life commands you to stay home, change your manners and attitudes in a positive way, and respect the ecosystem and any organism that exists in this world. Capitalism and other power systems may rule and control the world and to develop mechanisms to change a justice system against humankind.

During this difficult time, people are willing to be more spiritual and peaceful-minded. Believe in a higher power; it can give you an opportunity to see life in a different way. I pray and meditate to receive an alignment of wisdom. This certain intelligence may show me how to choose the right way to reach and focus on the bright side of life. On the other hand, some people believe that we have abused the environment and ecosystem by destruction of nature and that this is responsible for COVID-19.

This is a truth: human activities cause a health risk to a natural environment. We invade tropical forests, killing animals, cutting trees, and destroying the green landscapes to build high-rises and create global pollution from traffic in different environments. As a human being, I feel responsible for any creature in the world.

We can blame ourselves for generating this chaos. No one knows definitively when we can end this problem.

According to Abraham Hicks (a group of entities that are interpreted by inspirational speaker Esther Hicks), the most powerful topics are the following:

- health
- self-love
- parenting
- manifesting
- relationships

Affirmations from Abraham Hicks and Louise Hay taught me how to be empowered and strong during my tough life.

SOLUTION

The world is changing; all lifestyles have been changed. We will alter the world to begin life again with a new experience.

The Message of Love

I COME FROM A TRADITIONAL Iranian family that values a submissive daughter, a faithful wife, and a dedicated mother. I was not allowed to talk about my dreams. A woman in Iran is dependent on her family; she is not permitted to make decisions for herself. In fact, her family determines her future. There was no discussion between me and the members of my family about my future. I realized that upon graduating high school, I would get married and become dependent on my husband and my new family.

During the war between Iran and Iraq, I lost both my brothers. Unfortunately, my power of gratitude did not sufficiently keep my faith in God. I lost my motivation and my belief system. I just wanted to run away from the current circumstances. I became agnostic and wanted to start a new life, based on my unwilling belief.

My beliefs attracted a spouse who had the same beliefs as I had. There were no dreams for me to follow, and my future was certain. That began to change, however, as I grew as a person and started to realize my value in the world. When I turned nineteen, I got married and thought that I was mature enough to become independent by finding a job and going back to school.

In 1979, an Islamic revolution took place in Iran. The universities were closed, and women were not allowed to pursue degrees anymore. Consequently, I was not able to continue my education. I was confused and unhappy in my life until one night when I woke up in the middle of night and could not breathe. It was as if there was something inside my mind, controlling my body. I was numb and not able to move. It was like trying to scream while underwater. I had similar nightmares for a long time.

After I'd been married for a couple of months, I became pregnant with my first baby. I was excited and could not believe that there was a baby in my belly. Perhaps, though, it was not the right time for me to be joyful about becoming a mother.

An incident happened when I reached to turn on the light in the bathroom and touched a wet plug. This caused me to lose consciousness. The next day, when I opened my eyes in the hospital, the doctor told me that I had lost my baby. I was terrified and distressed. I could not believe that I had lost a living being. The doctor told me I should wait for a year before trying to have a baby.

After three years, I finally became a mother. I was in bed for eight months and two weeks while expecting my twin boys. I was extremely happy because one of my dreams was coming true. After all I had been through, I knew that my precious twin sons were special gifts from my dear God. I was responsible for doing my best to raise my beloved twins.

I had a new job—raising two beautiful sons and nurturing them with all that was within me. It was during this time that I began to read a variety of books and articles about psychology. The information in psychology journals helped me raise my children in a healthier way. When culture clashes occurred, I understood how to deal with my sons by observing their behavior and finding patterns. Not only did I find solutions and answers to my problems as a mother but I also found I had a very deep passion for psychology.

In fact, my motherhood experience gave me a wonderful opportunity to build up my self-esteem. Through this experience, I could open my eyes to a new world, and I realized that if I worked hard, I could achieve whatever I dreamed of, regardless of my family, culture, or prewritten future.

In 1996, time became available for me to go back to school, and it was very exciting. Things were not so smooth, however, as a similar pattern started when I began my educational career. When I got to school, my husband and I decided that biology would be my major so that I could become a dentist. I tried to finish the basic courses while working for almost ten years in my husband's dental office. I fell into the same trap of someone else making decisions for my life, and that's when I realized that our relationship was based on a conditional love—that I was expected to obey him.

For instance, he expected me to become a doctor if I wanted to live with him. He was not concerned about what I wanted personally. Coming from a male-dominant culture, it was difficult for me to break away from that. I realized that although it was a big step for my husband to even encourage me to earn a degree, he was only interested if I studied what he wanted me to study. In my heart, I knew what my passion was, but I did not dare speak about my interest in psychology. At that time, I thought that having the opportunity to pursue a degree was good enough.

But I had a strong urge to study psychology; I could not avoid it. After taking several psychology classes and studying psychology in relationships, I realized how unhealthy our marriage was. In the end, I divorced him.

I am grateful that I chose this profession. It has given me the ability to change my own life. I realized this was the career I wanted for the rest of my life because it had nurtured and guided me from motherhood to become an independent thinker. In my educational experiences, I learned how to change myself. I was not raised to stand up for my rights or to tell people no. I didn't tell people that I was interested in psychology and wanted to be a family therapist. It was just too odd and too frightening to go against what was familiar to me.

As a result, against my personal beliefs, I finished my college degree in biology. I learned a valuable lesson from completing my biology classes. First, I put value in finishing what I started, even if it wasn't what I wanted. Second, it was very important for me to pursue something that I *loved*.

I recognized that working hard for a meaningful future came a lot easier than working hard at something I did not want. After that, I told my husband that I wanted to transfer to California State University, Fullerton, to study psychology and that I was done with biology. He was in shock. So was I, as I couldn't believe that I was finally doing something that I loved. However, my mission was not finished yet. I still had a long way to go.

In order to improve my academic performance, I took some courses to develop my knowledge. I graduated with a degree in psychology from Cal State, Fullerton. I was excited to get my MFT (Marriage and Family Therapist) degree from Argosy University. And I continued my career, graduating in 2016 from Grand Canyon University's master's program.

Today, I realize that the value of education is powerful. This value belongs to me, and nobody can take it away from me. The power of education shaped me into an independent person; it also gave me everything that I wanted.

My future goals are to assist people who are like me. I knew that I was capable of working hard and finishing school. One of my lifelong dreams is to start a nonprofit community to provide support for the elderly with mental health disorders and disabilities, like dementia and Alzheimer's disease. I have researched diverse categories in different age ranges. I am interested in working with elderly people because I believe I can offer the most care and passion possible to this group.

Overall, I know, from every single step that I have taken in my life, that I am a loving, caring, and positive person and that therapy is a great match for my personality. I can make many contributions to society as a psychologist. It's important to me that I give to others what psychology has given to me, which is a purpose in life.

Be determined and strong in your life. Find the right time, the right place, and the right person. When you want to talk to your family, your boss, or your people, find the right time because it is more productive to talk with them then; they will be ready to listen to you.

Be Like a Butterfly

ONE OF MY DREAMS WAS to write and express my feelings in the proper way. When I look back on my life now, I realize how much I missed my mother. Most of the time, I blamed myself for the long distance between us and for not being able to see her for such a long time.

After I lost my mother, I was left with a guilty feeling, so I thought of a way to resolve this. After I graduated from my master's program at Grand Canyon University becoming a professional clinical counselor, I decided to develop my skills in different populations, especially working with the elderly. I was eager to understand what they needed, and I wanted to become a voice for them in the future. It was a new day in my life, and I kept my promise to take care of the elderly and those with special needs. I quickly started working on my goal and gradually became experienced in the elderly population, understanding and focusing on their needs.

My fear, however, caused me to have difficulty in communicating with this elder group. I had lost my father when I was a child, and I could not bear to think about my mother getting old and passing away. However, I eventually was able to face my fears toward the aging.

When I was a teenager, I thought when people got old, they became ill and were useless and lonely all the time. I thought there would be no one to take care of me. But I was wrong. I realized I could develop my knowledge and my career in this area.

After five years of research regarding the elderly, I realized that being old means you are free of stress, and you will have plenty of time to explore everything about your personal life. I tend to do that by following my dreams. I can complete my bucket list to bring joy and peace into my life.

I was hired three years ago as a caretaker in a private home care for those clients with mental health disorders, such as major depression and dementia. This population generally is able to communicate, and I encourage them by asking questions, such as how they met their spouse or other loved one when they were young. I love to sit down and listen to their stories. I have learned several techniques for communication, and I'm pleased to hear them.

By writing a book, I will be able to train other caretakers for the elderly with different mental health issues, such as Alzheimer's disease, dementia, major depression, or codependency, and they can improve their health conditions step by step. My purpose is to assist the family and caregivers to inform them on how to treat them in their care.

The best way of care is to speak and handle the elderly with love and understanding and to use respectful manners. This specific care is based on a learning process, including using amusing games and memory activities for the elderly.

Perhaps by focusing on these tasks, the clients will be motivated to give more attention to their environment. This informative care will be accessed from the health care facilities in order to consider the elderly with more affection and respect.

SOLUTION

Learn about the experiences of others. Start a new life; be a free spirit, like a butterfly. Change in your life can move you forward to a better future. Being realistic is the best way to see where you stand in your life. I always pray to God that I will not be controlled by my ego. No matter what, I always am humble and modest toward others.

Ordinary Lives for Ordinary Family Framework

ACCORDING TO BOWEN AND KERR (1988), a genogram is a graphic symbol of a family system, a combination of at least three generations. Its purpose is to help people see their context in visual form; therefore, pivotal moments and notable patterns can be acknowledged and recorded. In fact, genogram theory may be the best method to recognize the role of the family system in our lives. This is extremely vital for the younger generation. The narration of family tends to teach various knowledge that persists in your life as a collection of memories, whether negative or positive.

My spouse's parents came from Iran. They were young when they got married. Joe was twenty-five years old, and Alison was sixteen when they started their new life together. Joe was educated, and his goal was to become a doctor. After a while, however, Joe found a job in the army in order to take care of his family. He was responsible and a protective husband in a positive way.

In 1945 in Iran, a man was still the breadwinner, and there was no opportunity for a woman to show her abilities and talents outside of the home. Therefore, Alison, as a kind wife and happy mother, stayed home and took care of their two sons and a daughter.

In 1953, Joe joined political groups in order to protect the people from the war and injustice. In 1965, Joe was arrested by the police and sentenced to five years because of his political status. During the absence of her husband, Alison took care of her children near her own family. However, when Joe was freed from prison, he was not allowed to return to his profession, and he became restless and felt incompetent.

Their beautiful life became one of violence, anxiety, and stress. Alison was a protective mother and could not tolerate this situation. Most of the time, she was sad and embarrassed to share her feelings with her family. Throughout that time, people did not believe in therapy and counseling; the elder family members took care of the family dilemmas. Joe was resistant and resentful and did not to listen anyone. Some of their friends did not want to put themselves in that relationship. This family needed someone to make them open their eyes and help them to see reality.

When I look back on my life, I realize that therapy can be vitally important for every family. For instance, genograms can collect and organize information and the initial history of the family. The history of Joe's family showed that he was born into a wealthy family and was raised by his biological parents. When he was fifteen years old, a tragedy caused him to leave home. While Joe was looking for a job, he met Alison's brother Mark, who became Joe's real-life teacher and helped Joe to finish school. I loved Joe because he was close to my father, and I considered him as a father. He was a strong and generous man who was willing to help and teach people how to become independent thinkers. For instance, he once offered the following quote: "Give a man a fish, and you feed him for a day. Teach a man to fish, and you feed him for a lifetime."

After a while, Joe found his profession in the military. Then, his friendship with Mark allowed Joe to become closer to Alison, his future wife. Mark established a good relationship within Alison and Joe. In fact, in this healthy triangle, Mark tried to remain free of emotions and asked them to live on their own. Mark always was optimistic and allowed them to resolve their problems on their own.

Joe and Alison's relationship improved, as Mark always was coaching their lives and helped them to develop new skills, and they worked on their situation every day.

The family, however, was extremely sensitive and emotionally attached and dependent on each other. Unfortunately, after a couple of years, they lost Mark. Joe and Alison were trying to survive by working hard. Their children became successful enough to become physicians but married the wrong people. Then, the entire family immigrated to the United States. As a result, the family entered treatment and therapy so their children's marriages would not end in divorce.

My ex-husband was the second child; we divorced fourteen years ago. Based on the Bowen family genograms, we might stop ourselves from repeating the mistakes our families made in the past.

SOLUTION

The family should talk decently to each other. The family should have respect for one another, especially for women. A couple should share their most important things together. Having a role model is one of the dynamics in meeting and associating with successful people who become mentors in our lives.

Angel's Whisper

DESPITE HELPING OTHERS, ESPECIALLY ELDERS, I needed to select a flexible job so I could interact and communicate with the elderly in person. In the summer of 2017, I found a job as a counselor, or social worker. When I'd had these types of positions previously, I'd mostly worked in case management, insurance, and administration. After a while, I was unhappy, as it didn't satisfy me or help me to meet my goal. I prayed to God to lead me and show me a better plan to be happy from the bottom of my heart.

One Sunday morning, I woke up and started to pray. I told God, "I know you always help me to make the better decision and plan for me. Please help me to find my way become happy and enjoy what I want."

I was working in different areas of mental health and with different age ranges. I was not interested in working with the elderly who suffered from dementia or any disability and mental disorder. It was beyond my power and ability.

Then the miracle happened; that morning, a lady from the home care agency found my résumé and called to invite me to an orientation as a caretaker. I was not excited by this; I knew that I was overqualified for that type of position.

Still, I believe that things happen for a reason, and after my conversation with the lady, I decided to go for the training and orientation. When I went there for an interview, I started to like it.

The agency was located at the beach, and I felt a positive energy. The atmosphere of the office was pleasant and peaceful.

When I had a conversation with my supervisor about the clients, I learned that they were lovely and fascinating. It took me a while to follow my heart in this part of my life.

That same day, I found a way to stay in that job to see how it went. I was reading a book about dementia and elders with disabilities. Step by step, I was able to contribute to different classes. Reading spirituality books helped me to identify my plan to shift to a positive dimension. The most important factor was learning how to be patient for what I wanted to do.

I believe life is a dynamic process to learn and teaches so many valuable things. The purpose of my life is to help people (and myself) to bring love and peace with one another. In fact, my mission was clear for me; I wrote of my experiences and skills to all family health facilities, home care agencies, nursing homes, and assisted living facilities. Overall, people seek ways to manage their own lives as receivers and givers to find balance on the wheel of life.

My goals were to choose a flexible job as a caretaker and to work with clients individually and be in touch with the elderly's needs. I have learned how to trust and respect life and to grow and achieve my success. The power of gratitude allowed me to love and to be loved. As a result, this flexible job encouraged me to communicate with people in different age ranges. Such a connection can help us to understand the meaning of the journey of life and how to be happy and in peace.

SOLUTION

Be organized and be able to manage your daily schedule. Be hopeful, and be happy to do whatever you love to do so that you are comfortable in your own skin, without any reservation. Believe in angels. The good people are angels.

Miracles Always Happen

IT DEPENDS ON YOU TO see miracles in your life. I will help you to believe in yourself and raise your faith and trust in a higher power.

I got married, had my twin sons, and immigrated to USA in May 1989. When I got married, I lived with my husband's parents, Alison and Joe. They had their own problems, but I could tell that they loved me, and I was always welcomed in their home. Alison became grandmother to other grandchildren as well. When I got pregnant, I stayed in bed for almost nine months, and she took care of me all the time. I will never forget her kindness.

After my divorce, our relationship remained the same. It is awkward, but I still visit her. As of this writing, Alison is eighty-five years old, and sometimes I still go to her place, and we talk together like in the old days.

Alison is a nice lady, and I treat her with respect. I remember her as a strong woman who shared and sacrificed her life for the family. She helped and supported people who struggled with financial difficulties. I have my twin sons now because of her; she took good care of me through my pregnancy. It's my great privilege to have been inspired by her and to have learned how to think about others, especially the elderly who lack support and loving care.

Alison took care of her disabled mother for eleven years. As I look back on her family record, I see that she could take care of her mother for such a long time. but also about helping others. Unfortunately, in Iranian culture, you cannot love yourself first; it means you're selfish and egotistical.

As a person, you need to love, respect, and nourish yourself so that you can love others. For a long time, I lived with that mentality of taking care of others first.

Alison accepted that abusive life for such a long time. She thought that was the way it was—that a man had the right to get angry at his wife, and she just had to give her husband space until he cooled down. I always asked Alison, "What about the woman? Who could calm down a woman?" We are living in the twenty-first century. A man and a woman should treat each other with respect, love, and compassion. They are supposed to become one, based on unconditional love.

Alison was a born mother. She was lost and learned that she had to play the motherhood role. In reality, she did not understand any more than that. In some part of her life, she was not able to imagine a dream of her own. In fact, Alison's character was damaged in her childhood. Her mother was extremely ill and could not function well. She lacked the ability to stay home and take care of the family.

Sweet Alison, therefore, decided that when she grew up, she'd become a dedicated mother. She did a good job and raised her children in the way she learned from the past. Unfortunately, in the older generation, many parents were not open-minded to the new ways of nurturing their children.

Those types of traditional parents believed that heritage was more important in raising the children. As a result of this mentality, the number of dysfunctional families increased. Today, parents have been seeking for a new mentality to change and raise the way is accepted into the society. On the other hand, parents hand over all their characteristics and traits to their children, just as they learned from their own parents or guardians.

I understand and am open-minded to simplifying my past. I can forgive myself first and then others. I think this is the modest way to move forward in life.

In the past, most women were naïve and weak. They did not know how to change their own circumstances. Alison was one of my role models, and my new job in her house was taking care of the kitchen and helping her to make food for every member of the family.

My goal was to be a good wife and a great daughter-in-law. In fact, I was following my husband's dreams, not mine. There were no dreams and no imagination left in my world for me to become an active person or to look forward to it. Alison was nice to me, but that was not enough. As a young woman, I wanted to grow and change my life through a progressive pathway.

I would give up on myself and to see the beauty of the world. I wish I could have learned from Alison how to enable myself to love myself. Life goes on. The more potential you have, the more you can make a difference in the way you live. I accepted that life was full of choices and that I am responsible for my mine by making conscious decisions.

SOLUTION

Be patient, be brave, and be able to stand up for your rights, with respect. Follow your own dreams.

The Reality of life

I BELIEVE WE ARE UNIQUE. We can master the peace of our higher power. This brilliant power is called God. It's greater than me; it's the power I am able to trust. It is the infinity of love, compassion, and serenity. In spite of this power of manifestation, I am able to enhance the level of my creativities. In order to realize that the world is the most important concept of the existence or reality.

Life has value and mostly is a mystery, but the present can be an exceptional time, and it's in our hands. It's our choice how to trust God. According to motivational author Louise Hay, before we were born to this universe, we selected our parents and our place, interests, and whatever we wanted for our lives.

In fact, we are born with contrast and intelligence, which reveals the orderliness and discipline of the universe by the power of God. Nothing is made accidentally, and everything happens for the reason. In this world, it is our choice whether to be happy or miserable. By our wisdom, we can choose the brightness or the darkness.

If you think rationally, certainly you will be a hero of your own story. It means living with purpose and acceptance and helping others to reach their goals in order to make the world a better place. One of the best tools is to be aware of yourself—to give love and to treat yourself with respect and care. You can create a vibration of positive energy and release this energy around you like a sweet perfume. I will clarify how to start because you are at a turning point of everything; you are going to reach love, and love is God.

In our collective subconscious, we are the same human being—same structure but with different codes and unique characteristics; we are all made of the smallest elements called atoms, which is made of protons, neutrons, and electrons. Therefore, as a masterpiece of the universe we will complete our mission based on our wisdom and choices. Then, after we have completed it, we can transform to another life. The right time and right place will arrived when our missions are terminated.

As long as you understand the purpose of life, this knowledge can take you to the right place. Based on your needs and your awareness of your consciousness, you may develop your talent and creativity and discover your intentions in order to receive the abundance of love, health, and wealth in your life.

I can't imagine life without God. I will repeat: everything happens for a reason.

When I lost my two brothers as a teenager, I thought I had done something wrong and that God or the universe was punishing me by taking my beloved brothers from my life. I had hostility and resentment. There was no connection between God and me.

For a long time, I stopped giving myself love and stopped caring about my inner child—that part of me was forgotten. I surrounded myself with negative people. Sometimes I realized that something I was doing was wrong, but I could not control myself, and I repeated my mistakes.

After many years, miracles happened. I believe God has become closer to me than even my heartbeats. Wherever I go, I feel like someone is helping me to function well in my job. It makes everything easier for me, and it's joyful. I was seeking to stay happy without any reason.

Living in the moment can help you to aim for inner peace, and it allows you to feel positive vibrations. Make it a practice to add meditation to your life on a daily basis. By meditating, you can prove your readiness for a simple and a meaningful life. Your level of creativity could increase. Then, your mind gradually will become clear, and positivity can help to receive new dimensions of wisdom.

SOLUTION

The reality of life is a mystery. It is very complicated and is beyond your power. The power of anything in the world is God. God is love. Through your prayers, you can talk to him; with meditation, you can listen to God. Miracles happen in your life when you are open to your faith.

Care for You Because You Are Worth It

WHEN I GOT TO THE cemetery, Connie was there with a peaceful spirit. I brought her favorite flower—hydrangea.

In October 2018, she was still alive; she talked to me about her feelings regarding special holidays, like Thanksgiving and Christmas. She'd said she was always sad and felt lonely on each holiday. Connie knew that her doctor had given up on her because of her lungs and her heart condition.

Connie was not strong, and she lost her faith in prayer. She was not even interested in reading the Bible. I could understand her frustration regarding her illness and loneliness. I knew that Connie needed a professional to take care of her emotional and physical needs, someone who understood her feelings and could help her to chill out and relax. She needed someone who could invite her to calmness and inner peace.

If you believe in love, compassion, and kindness, you will attract the same type of people like an angel. According to the law of attraction, what you love, you empower. What you fear, you empower. What you empower, you attract.

I met my client Connie for the first time at her house. She was irritated and anxious to find a caretaker who could put up with her needs. Connie had a difficulty breathing and was always resting. She could barely use the stairs. Connie wanted to be alone in her life. In fact, there was something in her mind to keep her resentful. She was missed her absent family but she did not want to remember anyone from her past except her son. She was looking for someone to love her without any expectation. She was lonely, but throughout those days, Connie was able to experience a love connection with her caretaker and others. She also experienced prayers and forgiveness. Her stress and anxiety caused her to feel more pain in her broken heart. She wanted to stay in her own beautiful house forever. The collection of her memories encouraged her to keep living in her own place.

After I graduated with my master's program, I decided to work with the elderly. My main reason was because I wanted to help and communicate with this population. I wanted to learn how to take care of their mental and physical needs. My intention was to become a voice for them, with regard to what they needed to be happy and hopeful in their situations.

Over seventeen months, Connie became ready to connect with me and opened up her emotions. For instance, she didn't want to see herself in the mirror. She had a beautiful smile and still was beautiful. Because of her past, Connie's personal life crossed with her belief system. I asked her many times about her old photos because there weren't any pictures of her.

One day, I saw a beautiful picture of her at age twenty-three— scattered on the garage floor amid the broken frame. I cleaned that photo and showed it to Connie. She smiled and explained the story of that old photograph. Connie wanted to be alone and didn't want anyone to bother her while she was watching her favorite TV show.

Maybe she didn't want to expose her feelings from the past. She thought she was a leftover and that no one cared about hearing her stories about her life.

As a caretaker and a therapist, I was able to build up her trust and have healthy communication within Connie. After a while, Connie realized that she was capable of becoming a giver and a receiver of love.

I couldn't believe how soon this client became a lovable person. She gradually was motivated to read her mystery books, and she got ready to retake the written exam to renew her driving license, although Connie promised me that she wouldn't drive alone. She was happy and did some personal work by herself in order to enjoy her independence in life.

When Connie was a young lady, she always wanted to become an interior designer. She collected antique china or pieces of furniture. She subscribed to *Victoria* magazine to inspire more designs from the eighteenth century. Connie was created and made so many beautiful things around her house. She almost was perfect and professional when she wanted to learn baking, sewing, cooking, playing piano, reading books, gardening, and, of course, designing her house.

I could tell she had her own unique style. I called her Martha Stewart. In her kitchen, she designed part of the countertop like a bakery. When she was young, she baked her own bread, bagels, and cakes from scratch. She would wake up early in the morning and go to the kitchen to make a delicious breakfast for her family.

Every time I was in her kitchen and provided food for her, I imagined her in the kitchen, making a delicious meal. Sometimes, I took her downstairs and made food by following her recipe. We would eat together and have a good time.

SOLUTION

Life is a learning journey. We are always teaching and learning at the same time with one another. As a result of having Connie in my life, we learned and taught each other. It was a great experience for me.

Month One of My Job

ON THE FIRST DAY OF my job, Connie talked to me. She knew I was overqualified for the position, but she convinced me and understood my main reasons for selecting this flexible job. I couldn't take care of my mother because of the long distance and the war situation. After my mother passed away, I promised myself that I would take care of as many as grandmothers that I could and would treat them like my mother. Connie was impressed after she heard my stories. She smiled and told me what I could do for her—to feed her and stay there as a companion.

After a while, Connie was so happy and excited, but she didn't show any reaction. I wasn't allowed to talk to her while she was watching TV. After a while, we built trust between us and she believed me, and we talked about many subjects. She was looking for a daughter, and I was looking for a mother. A great bond grew between Connie and me.

Her housekeeper cleaned the entire house every other week, and we always ate together, making a nice picnic on her beautiful balcony behind her bedroom. The caretaker had established quality time and created a peaceful atmosphere around the house. The gardener and her cleaning lady were able to do their own jobs very neatly and nicely.

Every Friday, I tried to take a tour of her house with her. I asked her to talk about her beautiful memories with her family. She was not ready to tell me anything about her past because she'd become so anxious.

During the first week of my job, Connie was sad, but after a while, she got used to my being there every morning, and I would make her a big breakfast—two boiled eggs, toast with butter, a piece of cake, and a cup of coffee.

Every morning, I picked just one hydrangea from her garden and added it to her breakfast tray. Connie always was amazed by anything I did for her. I just wanted her to be happy and be assured that she was safe. I treated her like my mother, giving her love and attention, so she could see herself in the cozy, warm, and secure place called home.

We felt comfortable around each other. After her breakfast, we watched her favorite TV show. Then she would take a short nap before her lunchtime. I took her to her bedroom and encouraged her to read the bible. Then we meditated for fifteen minutes to be alone with God and to pray for peace in her family.

SOLUTION

Learn to trust people. Just be patient.

Month Two of My Job

IT WAS CLOSE TO THANKSGIVING and Connie's family wanted to visit her. She asked me to make a reservation at the best restaurant at the beach for her and her family on Thanksgiving. I suggested paying for the restaurant's bill by using the bucket of coins she'd been collecting for a long time.

The following day, we went to the store and cashed in her old bucket of coins. I had her help me drop the coins into the change machine, and she collected $250. She was happy and appreciative for what I'd suggested to her. She hugged me and said, "Thank you for coming into my life."

I smiled at her. "Any time, ma'am."

Thanksgiving arrived, and Connie was ready to meet her family at the restaurant. Later, she told me she'd had an amazing time with her son and daughter-in-law.

SOLUTION

Give people as many chances as you want.

Month Three of My Job

ON THE WEEK BEFORE CHRISTMAS, I picked up Connie to take her to see the Christmas ceremony and demonstration of the history of the birth of Jesus Christ at her neighborhood church. She enjoyed the outing, and thanked me for taking her to see the beautiful events of the Christmas. That night was one of her most amazing nights ever.

Caretaker tend to focus on the clients' needs. The caretaker is responsible for providing comfort for their clients and a safe place to stay, be calm, and relax. Sometimes, a caretaker asks the client to change her environment by going out for a walk or doing other activities outside. Clients have been encouraged to become more sociable and to connect with nature by breathing fresh air and doing daily exercise; this helps to improve their moods and promotes rational thought.

One of the caretaker's jobs is to check the client's medication and to learn about each pill the client takes—for example, learning the reasons for use and the benefits of the clients' medications. Clients would love to know about any difference and change in their personal lives. The caretaker might record any little thing in the client's file, such as the nutrition she takes.

Connie did not want to gain weight, so she always told me, "Please, no more sugar, fat, or carbs." Her doctor, however, recommended that she should eat everything but in small portions. I would provide three meals a day for her. I made a schedule for her meals, exercise, massage, and persona meeting, like taking a bath while listening to piano music.

I made her dream came true; she was looking for comfort and staying in peace in her own life. I played different roles—daughter, caregiver, nurse, masseuse, and therapist. I would understand that what she really need through her daily bases. I helped my client to find her place in life.

Connie was seeking love and was hopeful of getting better. Sometimes, she had an anxiety attack and had a hard time breathing. I learned to check and clean the filter on her oxygen tanks to make sure she could receive enough oxygen to her respiratory system. Mostly, she was happy to see me when I came to take care of her. She knew I was there for her, no matter what.

Connie had a beautiful sense of humor, and sometimes, she made me laugh so hard. On the day we met, Connie couldn't pronounce my name, but she wanted to remember it. She then asked me to say my name.

I smiled and said, "I tink my name—"

She stopped me and asked, "What did you say?"

I said "I tink—"

She stopped me again. She was excited and said, "That's it. From now on, I will call you *Tink*."

I grinned at her. "Whatever."

Connie kept calling me Tink—and when she was in a good mood, she called me *Tinkerbell*—but after that day, I eventually learned to pronounce *think* properly. The good point was that, little by little, I changed her perspective on Middle Eastern countries, certainly Iran.

SOLUTION

Learn social skills and have fun.

Month Four of My Job

JANUARY WAS END OF THE holidays, and life returned to normal. Connie felt better and was in a good mood. After being on the job with Connie for four months, she still had a problem with me and others. The good thing about Connie was that she knew her attitudes often got out of control. My job as a caregiver and a therapist, however, was to take care of her and be responsible for her needs. Sometimes, clients want me to keep them busy and have a nice conversation, to laugh, and improve their moods and help them to become peaceful.

Due to the stages of grief, clients often are not able to forget a dead loved one. Letting go can be difficult. Connie had lost her husband and could not to say goodbye to him.

Due to her mindset, she often was depressed and angry—two of the stages of grief. However, as a therapist and caretaker, I was responsible for helping her to reach the acceptance stage, even while she was not in a good mood. The stages are as follows:

1. Denial: Connie's illness changed her life, as she became dependent on someone to take care of her at least five hours a day. After a couple of years, she finally agreed with her son to sign up for home care assistance to receive services from a caregiver.

2. Anger: Sometimes Connie was angry about her life. She was restless and frustrated with putting up with her life situations.

3. Bargaining: She was under pressure, and her fear and anxiety level allowed her to become more ill and fatigued. Then she would ask, "Why me? Why did God put me in this situation?"

4. Depression: Mostly, she wanted to take a sleeping pill and stay in her bed all day to ignore her pain. She was frustrated and hopeless of her future.

5. Acceptance: Finally, through these times of her illness, she moved into the acceptance stage. After a while, Connie realized that she ought to face reality and look forward in her life as much as she could.

When optimistic people have a problem with regular daily schedules, they often would like to get through the grieving stages and concentrate on the acceptance stage. It's a great practice to understand profoundly the concept of any problem in life situations. Reaching the acceptance stage means shifting awareness and the level of the wisdom.

As a therapist, I believe when you have a certain problem on a daily basis, you would face the grieving stage all the time. However, the concept of the grieving will prompt you to reach the acceptance stage quickly and to stay at that stage.

Connie needed a companion to spend time with her. I was with her every day except Sundays; she didn't want me to get so tired that I would quit my position. I was concerned about her and wanted to keep her happy and hopeful in her life. I worked on her to become an independent and strong lady.

Connie irrationally feared that I would quit and leave her alone. Most of the time, we kept her busy, and she learned how to cope with her pain.

SOLUTION

Keep yourself busy and hopeful. Talk to God, and ask him for advice. When you have faith all the time, you will be happy without any particular reason. Stay away from fear, and love yourself so that you can love others. Stay away from irrational thoughts.

Month Five of My Job

CONNIE WAS HAPPY TO SPEAK with someone sometimes. She wanted to buy something for herself and went shopping with me; we also went to the doctor and to a nail solon. Occasionally, I took her out to see the town. It was hard for her to walk I wanted to take her for a walk in her wheelchair to see her neighborhood in different seasons. We each had good and bad days.

She sometimes became frustrated with trying to get enough oxygen in her body. Then she would argue with me for no reason. One day, she went to bed early and asked me to leave. I wasn't sure what to do. I knew a side effect of her medication was a change in her behavior.

I left her that afternoon when she told me to go. It was earlier than usual, and I couldn't stop thinking about her. Finally, I decided to get her favorite lunch and return to her place. I turned on the TV and set her lunch on her small table; then, I called her to eat her food.

She was still in her bed, so I said, "Hello, Connie. I got lunch for you. Would you be my guest? Come and eat."

Connie was upset about her earlier attitude. She looked at me, smiled, and said, "Please don't leave me. I'm sorry. I didn't mean to hurt your feelings. Please don't take it personally when I get mad."

"It's OK. No worries," I said. "Eat your meal before it gets cold. Let's talk about it tomorrow."

Connie smiled and said, "OK, see you tomorrow."

SOLUTION

When you respect yourself, you will be able to respect others. You teach people how to treat you.

Month Six of My Job

IN MARCH 2018, CONNIE WAS almost happy, but she was reserved and reluctant to express her emotions. Life is complicated, and sometimes, we don't have the patience to deal with our lives. Connie became physically weak and didn't want to speak because her heart could not function properly to receive enough oxygen. I was responsible for filling her pillbox every Friday to make sure she was fine with her medication on a daily basis. Sometimes, she missed her medication on the weekends.

I took her to the doctor to get his opinion on her situation. I was watching her diet to make sure she was eating a healthy food. I believe healthy food can change one's mood in a healthy way, and I enjoyed taking care of her.

Every Friday, I gave her a bed bath, and I changed her clothes every other day. I was able to give her a bath after I bought her a chair so she could sit comfortably when I washed her body. Then, we would listen to soft music, like piano music, while I massaged her with lotion. Connie enjoyed the way I pampered her. She always told me, "I can't imagine life without you."

When I saw that I made her happy, I wanted to do every favor for her. She expressed her feelings and always showed her appreciation. She started to pray again at night.

Month Seven of My Job

THE WEATHER WAS HOT, AND Connie was happy to have me there for a couple of hours to keep her company. We had fun when she was in a good mood. After a couple of months, she learned to trust me and others. When Connie was alone and had pain, she tried to use painkillers to help her sleep. The next day, usually a Monday when I got back to work, she would be confused and frustrated and always thought someone had broken into her house.

By my talking and listening to her, she calmed down and asked for her breakfast. After her breakfast we would make plans to go to her doctor, and after that, she often invited me for lunch. Every other Friday, we had a picnic at her house with her cleaning lady.

Gradually, Connie learned to become more sociable and to talk more with the people around her.

SOLUTION

The power of love made her strong and independent. She wanted to listen my stories. Sometimes she worried about my life, but I always told her, "I have God."

Month Eight of My Job

IT WAS MONDAY, AND CONNIE had an appointment with the cardiologist. I prepared everything we needed for the road. The doctor was satisfied after she checked Connie; everything was under control. We followed the doctor's directions on what Connie needed to do.

After that, we went for a quick lunch at the beach. Sometimes, I wanted to invite her to lunch as my treat. Connie enjoyed the view of the ocean, and she learned to talk about the beauty of the nature. She showed her appreciation for what she saw outdoors.

At the end of the day, she went to bed and slept in peace, getting ready for another beautiful day.

SOLUTION

She was confident in doing her personal job. She was happy.

Month Nine of My Job

CONNIE FINALLY SEEMED HAPPY FOR me to stay with her. She stopped reading mystery books and watched fewer programs with negative news. I could tell her attitude had changed and her interests were reformed. One of her new experiences was meditating for fifteen minutes before her naps.

One day, when she woke up from her nap, she took me to her one of her rooms and showed me her different handkerchiefs and very beautiful pillow cases. She had sewed and designed all those fabrics. Connie dreamed that in setting up a fund-raising campaign by selling her favorite needlework collections, she would be able to donate money to save many lives in Mexico. It was one of her plans; she supported different organizations that helped orphans. Connie was concerned that everyone should be safe.

Through her daily meditation, Connie was able to clarify her thoughts and receive the right resolution and growth in her life.

SOLUTION

She learned how to meditate and listen to God.

Months Ten to Fifteen of My Job

DURING THESE MONTHS, CONNIE'S SITUATION in life was mellow and went smoothly forward. Connie was OK, and in the middle of autumn, she started to open up. She asked me to clean and collect her family photos into boxes. Connie said that after she died that I should hand those boxes to her children. She also typed a meaningful letter for her family, in which she talked about the great memories and said thank you for what they had done for her. Connie attached the beautiful portrait of her when she was young. By the end of her story, I learned that she had been a model when she was young. Connie was pleased and felt free.

SOLUTION

She learned to respect her memories of her past.

Love to Be Loved

DURING THOSE MONTHS THAT I cared for Connie, she became very emotional and sensitive. There were two different and competing sides to her. Mostly, she forced herself to accept the way she was, and she walked on eggshells in her life because of her feelings of doubt.

I always believe this phrase: Stop changing and controlling others. Start changing and reforming yourself; then your positive energy will affect everyone around you.

The alternative tools are to show your action and prompt others to become observers and learners in their own lives. For instance, I focus on my clients' needs. It is essential that I make clients happy and comfortable while I am around them.

I find a great personal aspect of the clients in order to communicate and interact with them. When I met Connie, for example, the first thing I loved was her beautiful smile. She was quiet and private, but after a while, she realized that I was a lovable and trustworthy person with whom she could communicate.

As a therapist, one of my aspirations is to influence my clients through love and being loved, often as a giver and a receiver. When I was a little girl, my mother was overly protective of me. She kept telling me, "God is watching what you're doing."

I was a child and didn't understand what my mother said about God. That mentality allowed me to be misled in the way I was. The fundamental of this misunderstanding caused me to be ashamed of my femininity as I grew up. I thought it was a sin to see myself naked in the mirror. After a long time, my perspective of my belief in God shifted and gradually became stronger and keener.

There is abundant foundation of peace and serenity created in my heart—the amazing feelings of connection of the infinity of loving affection, which is received from the power of God. This loving affection can encourage me, not only by showing value, respect, and devotion in my life but also by showing support and by devoting my life to the people who deserve to love and be loved.

After all the time I spent with Connie, we had an opportunity to get to know each other better. Connie was able to forgive herself and others. She had a chance to make a peace with herself and her family. She was also enabled to express her feelings and say "I love you" to her son and others. Connie had a big heart but because of her painful past, she did not learn how to be patient or to compromise in her life situation.

When she got sick, she needed someone to take care of her and provide her comfort in her daily schedules. Connie had a heart bypass operation, and her lungs had less than 50 percent function. She had difficulty breathing, and she always used a nasal cannula to deliver supplemental oxygen.

In reality, her cardiologist and her primary physician had given up on her. They told her she would live no longer than six months. Connie could not accept any caretaker to take care of her. She was overwhelmed by seeing any stranger in her house.

I believe that in this world, nothing happens accidentally.

I was seeking a counseling position to work in my field of psychology. Then, one Sunday morning, I had a telephone call from the Home Care Assistance Agency—the supervisor had found my résumé online, and she thought I could be a great match for clients who needed to work through grief and who needed companionship. The supervisor listened to my story about my mother and convinced me to work with them.

I decided to accept the position; I would make myself calm by helping the elderly and treating them like I had treated my mother. It was great therapy for me at that particular time in my life.

At the same time, I was looking for love and for a mother figure on whom I could rely and who would nurture me like my own mother—and then Connie came into the picture. When I met Connie, I was so happy; I felt I could see my mother's smile on Connie's face. That day, we became like angels for each other.

As I've mentioned, Connie said I was overqualified for the job, but after I told her my story about my mom, she became emotional and expressive—actually, we both were emotional. We had found each other at the right time. Her face seemed very familiar to me, as if I had known her for a long time.

SOLUTION

Life is short. It's not worth it to be resentful over some problems. We shouldn't judge anyone. We may not understand or like people the way they are, but we cannot change them. However, we may change ourselves, and we may be good role models for them if they decide to change.

Connie Said Goodbye to this World

FALL WAS AROUND THE CORNER, and Connie was happy that her son and daughter-in-law were coming for a visit. Connie made so many plans for that day, and she shared each new plan with me. One day, however, Connie told me that they could not visit her after all. Something had come up, and they could not make it for Thanksgiving.

The holiday became stressful for Connie. When Thanksgiving arrived, I decided to take coffee and Connie's favorite breakfast to her house. We had a good time together. I was there until three in the afternoon, and then I left her house to spend Thanksgiving with my friends.

The following next week, when I got to her house, she was very weak; I could tell she was not OK. I called 911 and they took her to the ER, where she stayed for a couple of days. When I visited Connie, she barely remembered me.

She was taking a lot of medication, but Connie asked me to take her back home. She asked to be discharged by her own permission. I promised to take her home and to bring the hospice workers to her house for her care. The LVNs and RNs came in different shifts.

There was not any improvement for Connie. Every time I saw her, she seemed to be getting worse. For three weeks, I stayed with her from 8:00 a.m. to 8:00 p.m. I finally called her family, and her son came and stayed about two weeks with his mother.

One Friday evening, as I was about to leave Connie, I hugged her and held her cold hands. She was still in a coma and struggling with her life.

I whispered to her, "Connie, imagine you are in a peaceful place. There is a beautiful garden, full of the roses and hydrangeas. You are waiting to go into the garden, but it's not time yet. Just be patient, Connie. You will be there. You're having very beautiful feelings right now. You are so pleased to see your loved ones.

"You are free now. There is no pain. You are in the light channel and can see and touch love with tenderness. You have become young, with beautiful skin, like a baby. Very soon, you will fly—no worries. We are going to be OK without you. Go forward and don't come back home. There's nothing here but pain, loneliness, and sadness remaining for you. Go on toward the inner peace. We do not need you here. I want you be happy and show me your beautiful smile."

While her eyes were closed, Connie squeezed my hands and smiled.

That night when I went to bed, I had a beautiful dream about Connie. Her face was on the top of a full moon, and it was very close to my eyes. She was smiling and looking at me.

I said to her, "Hi, Connie. Go to the light. You are free now."

Suddenly, I saw my mother in my room. She got up from the armchair, smiling at me, and flew back to the sky next to Connie's face. Both faces became one. The face smiled and waved at me, while they flew at the speed of light.

On December 15, 2017, at 10:00 p.m., the home care office texted everyone to announce their client, Connie S., had passed away, with peace.

SOLUTION

My memories of Connie always will remain in my heart. I am delighted that she had a good experience with me.

My Journey

AFTER CONNIE PASSED AWAY, I made a plan to work on my goal and see what I should do for my life. Would I keep this position and help the elderly or do another job, like counseling? I needed a break; I was burned out because I missed my mother and Connie. My family understood that I was emotionally involved with my job. They realized that I was responsible for what I was doing and that this involvement was worth more than a job.

Before I returned to my job, I decided to get away from town and travel with my family and also on my own. During those months, I had the most amazing experiences, and everything became extremely clear to me. After sixteen years, I planned to visit my brother and his family in the UK. Throughout the time I was in England, I just wrote, and there was a plenty of time to spend quality time, alone and with my brother. I was so happy that, after such a long time, I could see my family.

After I returned home, I was determined to stick to my plan of helping people as much as I could. I wanted be a better person; that's the way I tend to run my life. My dream came true. I could hear the whispers of miracles.

There was no fear, no negativity, and no sadness. All my feelings were compassion and trust. For the first time, I started to believe in myself. My faith showed me the power of love and positivity. The alignment and affirmations allowed me to continue my mission of helping people, especially the elderly. My willpower told me to write and share my creativity and skill with all people, my family, facilities that treat those with Alzheimer's and dementia, nursing homes, rehab facilities, and home care.

SOLUTION

If you want to do so, take a break and travel before making a final decision. During travel, you can relax and have time to think about your plans and goals for the future. You will meet new people, and you will learn and teach at the same time. It is an enriching experience.

Hello, Lovely Sue

AFTER I RETURNED FROM THE UK, I felt refreshed and full of energy. The home care agency assigned me for a couple of hours in assisted living for patients with dementia. The facility was very beautiful and was perfect for patients with dementia.

My client was fifty-five years old; she was very nice and beautiful. It was her first day, and she was nervous and impatient. She had a dog with her, Mosley, and she kept asking the same question.

Her husband had placed her in assisted living and left her there; he had difficulty in keeping his wife at home. My client kept looking for her husband so she could return home. It was really heartbreaking for her to stay in this facility when she had a twenty-year-old son and a husband. I did not have any experience with working with patients with dementia.

I was sure there were many skills and tools I would need to work with this type of patient to have a better communication with her. After I left the facility, I promised myself that I would become the patients' voice.

As a result, I realized it was important for me to learn and develop new skills to achieve my goals. I went for special training and read as much information as I could.

SOLUTION

Collect new skills and new experiences.

Love is Magic

AFTER I DIVORCED, I WAS able to purchase a beautiful and cozy condo. I decided to remodel my condo the way I wanted. My twin sons were living with me. They were students, and I provided their own rooms in my new place. After all that we had been through over the years, we now were able to develop a peaceful environment full of love, energy, and positivity.

My sons and I were studying under the same roof, and we all graduated our undergrad programs in the same year. My dreams came true. Life is love. Believe that if you have good feelings and positive vibrations about anything, you can aim toward it without any reservations.

The law of attraction is the best way to get you where you want to be. It has been about thirteen years. Now I am by myself and free of stress. There is nothing wrong in imagining and dreaming for what you really want.

God always was there for me and took care of me when I called him. The power of gratitude can allow you to live in the abundance of love, happiness, inner peace, health, and wealth.

ABUNDANCE OF LOVE

By taking good care of yourself with love, you can invite value, respect, and peace into your heart.

MEDITATION

By this method, you can get away from negativity, irrational thoughts, and useless information in your mind. Meditation can help you to generate your creativity, knowledge, and wisdom.

ABUNDANCE OF HAPPINESS

When you love yourself and have good feelings in your heart, then you will feel inner peace and be happy in your heart. You will love to help people. In fact, it gets easier for you to forgive the people who hurt your feelings in the past.

ABUNDANCE OF HEALTH

The tendency of positivity may let you scan your body and be grateful for every healthy cell you have. While you are meditating, focus on your body. Imagine your body is a powerful factory that will carry all the packages to the right place, without any postponement or delay. The beauty of this process is that it has been programmed, and you cannot do anything to interfere with your body system. Hence, the only thing you should concern yourself with is taking care of this organism. When you check what you eat and search for the right food, you can keep your youth and health forever. Aging will fade from your life. Also, by working out and exercising, you can build up a great harmony within your bodily functions. It makes a huge difference when you follow this healthy schedule.

ABUNDANCE OF WEALTH

The power of gratitude teaches you how to manifest a lot of money. First of all, learn the value of money. Money is for your comfort; thus, keep some cash in your purse or wallet, and touch the money, fold it, and put it in order.

Learn to save money. For instance, when I am doing laundry in my home, I see coins everywhere, especially on top of the dryer. Previously, I didn't know what to do with that spare change. One day, I used my creativity and decided to collect all my change and keep it in a piggy bank. Then I could spend it for whatever I needed around the house.

Alternatively, make plan to save money for any purpose in your life, such as paying your debts, including your credit cards, or traveling. Manage your money by the power of gratitude and positive vibrations.

SOLUTION

Be open to new skills, and awareness will change your life. Stay away from being narrow-minded, judgmental, or biased.

Living in the Moment

SHOW RESPECT AND APPRECIATION FOR what you consume. Your subconscious could be encouraging you to change your life to a better structure. Love always is in the air, and you will feel inner peace and tenderness as you live within a love connection. You will be wedded with the universe and feel abundant love. In fact, the world will fit in your heart.

Love is recycled—if you understand it, you will receive an overflow and abundance of affection. Gradually, you will feel the change in your life. You will love to pay attention to nature and spend more time with your loved ones. You won't ever be in a rush or be late. The power of love and appreciation can teach you to see the world differently. For instance, this type of life, will help you to inform that every minute of your time has a value.

Life is learning process, and you have the choice to live the way you want. The purpose of life is to follow your goals, to create useful and interesting talents and skills. Afterward, your intention should be to resume your specific interests and consider them as a job or profession. Do your best, and be good in your own way. If you keep loving yourself, you will open all the possibilities in your life. A new day and new possibility can be coming to you. Start your regular schedule with a beautiful affirmation from Louise Hay or Abraham Hicks, the best motivational teachers on the planet. Set up the time, and keep track of your minutes with a timer until you go to work. Practice self-care, such as meditation, exercise, and getting ready for work.

HOW TO START YOUR DAY IN A PLEASANT WAY

1. *Meditation:* Start your day with meditation. Choose your favorite spot in your home, and meditate there for fifteen minutes. Sit up; then put your hands on your lap, close your eyes, and take a normal breath, Imagine yourself in the galaxy, the Milky Way, and you are in the light in the black holes of a hundred billion galaxies, profoundly moving into the darkness. You could be flowing in the deep dimness. There is no gravity, and you are a free spirit, flying everywhere you go. Ask yourself what you want from the universe. Just make a wish and visualize that you have your wish in your hands. Then give power to your imagination, and stay deeply in that moment. Keep breathing until your fifteen minutes is over.

2. *Exercise:* After meditation, doing some stretching for fifteen minutes, and get ready to walk for another fifteen minutes.

3. *Self-care:* Start your day with breakfast. The definition of *breakfast* is to break your fast (stop fasting). Thus, a healthy breakfast is vital, including eggs, avocado, cottage cheese, honey, dates, grapes, gluten-free bread, walnuts, and almonds. You can choose a couple of these items every day. Manage your time so you have fifteen minutes to enjoy your breakfast without any rush. By loving and respecting your body, you can assume that healthy food will keep you in a good mood and better shape.

When I worked with children, they had to learn how to enjoy their meals at lunchtime. I would create different games for the children who did not eat sufficient food; somehow, they often skipped their lunches.

One game, for example, was this: Put a piece of strawberry in your mouth. Close your eyes and think about the beautiful garden where it grew. You see the farmers sitting on the ground, picking strawberries, one by one. It takes many steps to carry those strawberries to the store so that you can buy them.

This technique encouraged the children to eat while having fun.

SOLUTION

Life is beautiful. If you want to take advantage of time, focus on every single second. With everything you do—such as meditation, having meals, and doing exercise—use your timer to do your job effectively and slowly. By focusing on the time, you will enter into an abundance of time. You will be able to live in the moment and enjoy life for a long time.

We Are Like a Family

AFTER MY SONS LEFT HOME, I was in the denial stage of grief for such a long time. For seven years, I worked as a preschool teacher. I lived by myself, and the only thing I did was go home after work, lie down to watch TV, and go to bed. I did nothing for a while; I had no hope or motivation. There was a beautiful week when my sons came back home for a couple of days. We had fun together, but when they left, I was depressed for several days.

One weekend, I decided to make myself busy with gardening and decorating my living room. One of my hobbies was watching romantic and inspirational movies. I always paid attention to the dialogue in the movies and looked for any message I could receive. One movie I loved and watched every year was *Under the Tuscan Sun*, which is about a woman who is divorced and decides to change her life. She goes to Italy and visits Tuscany. Suddenly, she sees her dream house and purchases the old and beautiful house in Tuscany. She's alone, but she works hard to fix and remodel the house in the way she wants it to be.

At first, she's upset and lonely in her new place. She says to her neighbor, "I am alone, and I'm stupid to buy this house by myself."

"Why did you?" the neighbor asks.

"Because I'm tired of me being afraid all the time," she answers. "Because I still want things. I want a wedding. I want a family in this house."

"Part of this area was a mountain," the neighbor tells her, "and it was hard for the train to pass, but people built up the tracks for the train because they were hopeful; they knew that one day, the train would be coming."

I was amazed by their conversation about hope and having a dream. Yes, I wanted a family for myself. I got the house for my sons, but they were gone now. I didn't want them to give up their future because of me. I just wanted them to be happy and have their own dreams.

After a while, I decided to have my own family in my house. I wanted to have parties and hear people laughing in my house. I wanted to cook, garden, and go for walks together; watch movies and talk together. I was happy, and I could not imagine life as better than that. God always has helped me, and I know he has plans—better plans—for my life.

SOLUTION

The level of your compromise is high. You are a lovable person, and people love you and see you as part of their family. You are kind and caring. You help people and love people as you love yourself. You are so easy to love. You are willing to seek a solution, not a problem.

Care About You

THE MOMENT I MET SUE, I clicked with her. I believed that after Connie, this client was the one to fill her place for me. Sue was a quiet and caring lady who always smiled. Her sense of humor made me have more conversations with her. A couple of years ago, Sue had a stroke, which resulted in her being diagnosed with dementia. I had prepared myself to work with patients who suffered with dementia and Alzheimer's.

The new day arrived for me, and I treated Sue with love and compassion. Sue was eighty-one, and her stroke and her illness had affected her memory. Usually, on my first day with clients, I like to talk with them and tell them what I can do for their needs.

As a therapist and a caretaker, I want to create alternative ways for them to cope with their needs. Sue wanted someone be there and observe her, to make sure she was safe and secure. She needed me three days a week, for twenty-four hours each week. As a result, I added another client to my daily schedule in order to stay in this job and complete my projects and research of the elderly.

When I was in my forties, I didn't want to communicate or associate with anyone who was older than I was. I didn't like to think about aging and being old. I had issue with death; it was one of my weaknesses. I knew I had to face it and move on in order to grow and develop a new perspective.

Working with the elderly gives me an opportunity to find a new me, to see the reality and beauty of life. Before we leave this universe, we should complete our missions. It means that we will graduate from this part of our lives. As a result, we have a choice of the way we want to have existed.

As I started to work as a caregiver and therapist, I felt so comfortable in my own skin, without any reservation. This profession helps me (and I help others) to clarify the simplicity of life. It is very important for me to listen to my clients' stories; to hear them from the bottom of my heart; to communicate with them, ask questions, and make them laugh; and to respect them for who they are as human beings.

Being old means that you are almost there—at the peak. Spread your wings to fly; be free and light of weight. Being old means you are wise from your treasury of experiences. You are different, and that give you the benefit of traits and characteristics that create a magnificent harmony.

I feel good about myself and enjoy every moment of my life age. With this new affirmation, I decided to change my life and communicate with the elderly who have difficulties and are suffering from mental illness. The best healing for them is sending love and compassion. One of the great methods for care is laughing and encouraging amusement and a sense of humor and hilarity.

For example, one of my clients is Jain, who is over seventy-five years old. Sometimes, I take her to the store to buy what she needs for her household. One day we went to Costco, she was looking for trash bags but only found a box with five hundred bags.

"That's too many," she said.

Teasing her, I said, "Yes, it's too many. Even when you're one hundred years old, you'll still have those trash bags."

She smiled and said, "After I'm gone, I'll leave the bags for you."

Jain loves to laugh and have fun with her caregivers. Every week, she has a Bible study at her place. Most of the time, she and her neighbors engage in different activities, such as watching movies, having a potluck, playing games, or having book club. Jain also is active in church, helping people to improve their own situations.

Jain believes there is always a choice to have a beautiful life. "The simplicity and clarity of life allows you to focus on laughing, listening, loving, and learning," she has said. In fact, the magnificent factors of this experience can open a new chapter of life, one in which you can smile and normalize aging and make it work. Life is a matter of perspective. In reality, it depends on how you live. Jain loves to learn new skills to use her creativity and to make her life more useful.

Jain has surrounded herself with positive people who have fun, laugh, love, and help each other. Life is unpredictable and sometimes can be full of surprises that take you on a joyful and remarkable journey. The most important dynamic for this group is communication because they have plenty of time to talk and listen to you. They share their own experiences.

My best days are when I go to work and visit them. Jain always wants to listen to my new story. We like to talk and learn new things from each other. Jain is smart and a quick learner. She always shows her appreciation and gratitude for everything she owns. She's amazed by technology and excited by the way she can receive help from her Apple TV and cell phone. For instance, she wanted to use her alarm, and I taught her how to use her cell phone as an alarm clock. She is excited when she learns a new skill. She has taught me that if I help someone, I will get more in return. Jain once told me a touching story that I have never forgotten:

A woman was getting evicted from her home. Her house was in foreclosure, and the police left the notice for her to evacuate her house. She was unhappy and didn't know what to do.

While she was crying and packing to move, a young man knocked on her door. He said, "I purchased your house in your name. This house belongs to you again."

The woman was shocked and could not believe this miracle. The young man then explained that he had lost his parents years ago and had become homeless. Shortly afterward, he had met a woman on the street and had asked her for money.

She was concerned about him; he was so young to be taking care of himself on the streets. She got a loan from the bank and gave him half of her money.

The young man was surprised. "Thank you so much," he'd said, "but you don't even know me. How can I repay you?"

The woman smiled. "You don't have to repay me, but promise me that one day, when you get back on your feet, you'll help the people who desperately ask for help."

As he grew up, he followed his dream to become the top successful realtor in his town. One day, when he checked the list of foreclosures, he found the woman's name and decided to pay back her favor by purchasing her house. He paid it forward.

I was impressed by this story from Jain. No wonder she was healthy and happy at her age; she always lived in peace and helped to support people in need. In the past, when her husband was alive, they were active in church as a counselor. She believes that hearing and understanding people was a type of art psychology. She loves her social life and listening to people who need to talk.

I was lucky to find her companionships for eight hours a week. I just observe her to ensure that she's safe when she takes a shower. We have interesting conversations when we meet each other through the week. We have lots of things to share with one another.

I know that God always has a better plan for me. In this universe, whatever you are wishing for, you will be able to receive it. My purpose is to keep my jobs with the elderly.

I wanted to stay in touch with them individually, to watch them and communicate with them. Today, I have two wonderful clients, Jain and Sue. I see them separately, with different regular schedules. I talk with them, listen, and do certain activities, based on their own needs. While I am taking care of them, I can meditate and have free time to take care of other responsibilities.

When we awake every morning, we play different roles in our lives. For instance, a woman has different roles as a person, such as wife, mother, housekeeper, neighbor, boss, employee, driver, lover, and so on. When her husband needs help, she talks with him, and her role may change to mother. When he gets sick, her role may change to nurse or a caregiver. In healthy relationships, it's fitting when we play our roles properly.

On Valentine's Day, I worked with Sue. Dementia caused her to lose her short-term memory, but she remembered it was Valentine's Day. I got a big balloon and chocolates for her, and I made a special hot tea for her.

Every time elderly persons fall down, there can be damage in their brain cells, and that affect their memories. Sue fell on the floor and fractured her right shoulder.

She doesn't remember me every time we meet. I get her to say my name, and I tell her my routine schedule. Sometimes she was disoriented and asks about her town and her place. Sue is smart, and she gets frustrated when she can't remember where she is.

I like to help her and talk to her about her life situation. I describe her feelings and tell her, "Sue, you are absolutely right, and I can understand you how you feel. However, you had stroke, and your brain is functioning in a new way."

I used to get upset when Sue could not remember her day or what she did even a couple of minutes ago. Her mind isn't designed to remember new information.

But I am in the acceptance stage. I always want to keep myself in this stage—just accept the reality and the way it is. I am powerless toward the things that could happen in my life. It is not in my hands to change those who live around me. As a result, I accept new situations and use my creativity to learn more skills for communication with people. This helps to prevent me from controlling, judging, and assuming.

I open up to Sue and share this technique with her. Her new memory has been designed to focus on the present time, so I tell her, "Today is a gift. Enjoy your new beginning." Sue is a strong lady, and her logic may help her to address her new life. She has a great treasury of advice. As I've mentioned, the best thing about the elderly is that they have plenty of time to talk and listen to you with patience and compassion.

Sue loves to listen. She understands and remembers what you've said, and she asks questions if she doesn't understand you. She explains her opinions on the relevant dialogues. Sue's mind always is changing to different pathways. It depends on her mood. Mostly, she reminds herself when she repeats herself.

When Sue gets disoriented, I keep calm and answer her questions. I explain everything to her when she's confused. The logic and reasoning part of her brain is active, and she can understand the reason and the consequences of any issue; in fact, she knows the concept of cause-and-effect.

For instance, when she refuses to walk or get out of bed, I describe the benefits of exercise and walking for her health conditions. Her problem-solving and reasoning helps her to accept her life situations. The power of love allows you to admit and love people in the way they are. Sometimes, Sue does not remember me, but the important thing is, I remember her.

After a couple of months, things changed around Sue, but her situation remained the same. There was no improvement for her. I had the same schedule with her. As everything changed in her life, my treatment changed to a different pathway. I talked to her and told her different stories, and she was so excited to hear them. It was a great exercise for her to try to remember whatever I said. After a while, though, my job changed.

Sue was not able to move her body anymore, and she spent most of her day in bed. She lost her interest in playing games and listening to my stories. She wanted quiet, and her fun now became eating her meals and staying in bed. We had a short conversation, but she said she'd rather be alone. I would never leave her alone, even though she tended to go to sleep.

During Christmastime, she was happy to spend time with her family, but after a while, she would become tired. In the morning, after her breakfast, she would watch TV. Then we did exercise, and I gave her a sponge bath and deep hygiene. She just wanted to do these things faster so she could go back to bed and take a nap.

After all these days, Sue could not move and her condition was almost the same. Her blood circulation affected her balance so she couldn't sit by herself. She always needed assistance in standing up from her bed and walking. Her memory did not incorporate her next move. Sometimes, it was hard for me to lift her, and she was not comfortable when she watched trying to help her up by myself.

After a while, I decided to quit my job with Sue because I did not want to risk my health. It was difficult to say goodbye to her, but I had to do it. The last day of my job finally arrived, and I was ready to tell Sue about my problem.

It was a Saturday morning when I visited Sue. I was there on time;

she was awake and waiting for her breakfast. I just wanted to talk to her and spend more time with her. After a couple of hours, I told her that this was my last day. "I won't be able to come here again because I found out I have a back problem."

Sue was a very understanding lady. She smiled and said, "OK, sweetie. I will miss you, but it's a good idea to think about your future." I was glad she said that to me. At the end of the day, she looked at me and said, "I think it's time to leave."

I was not able to hug her because of social distancing measures.

SOLUTION

Sue is love, and she taught me how to love someone without any expectations. She always said to me, "Let your sons live, and leave them alone. They are free, and they will come back to you." She believed that love is magic and that we must love to be loved.

Change Your Thoughts with Blessing

CHANGE YOUR THOUGHTS; CHANGE YOUR life—this is one of the best affirmations in my entire life. You cannot change anyone, except yourself. When you are willing to change your thoughts, you can clarify your mind. In fact, this reality helps you to choose your goal. If you want to change someone you love, start with yourself, and leave the other person alone.

If you want your loved one to read a book as a new habit, start that habit yourself. Add reading a book to your regular schedule. Then, when your loved one sees you are serious about your new habit, he or she may be interested in asking questions about what you are doing. We can't control or pressure someone to do the same thing that we do on a daily basis.

There are different ways to meditate, and each receives different outcomes. One way is to clear your mind to stay in peace. The more you meditate, the more you will increase your creativity. When you improve your rational thoughts, you will have a chance to receive your dreams. I love to write down the things for which I am grateful.

Our job is to explore our abilities and interests. The moment we find our talents, we can focus and improve in the profession we love. When you love what you are doing, you will never tire of doing it. A joyful job encourages you to receive more success and accomplishments. Just use your power, and create something unique, without copying from anyone else.

Select a role model to show you the way of success, but look for your own skills and talents to become empowered and fulfilled.

The point is that we should responsible for our actions in order to build trust and integrity. Another point is that with the power of gratitude, you will deposit more blessings in your life. By resolving problems, you will be able to concentrate only on solutions. When fear goes out the window, bravery enters the door.

In my opinion, we are responsible for each other. Some people come into your life for a specific reason, and they stay in your life for a short time. This type of person is like an angel, showing up to help and support you; then the person disappears.

These people are willing to teach you a valuable lesson. After finishing their jobs, they will vanish, just like a guardian angel. Miracles always happen if you are grateful for everything you have. According to Sara Young (2012), counting your blessings means you will attract more abundance in your life. This is very interesting affirmation. If you follow the law of attraction, you will attract more blessings from God.

Every single day, count your blessings and use these magic words when you have a moment to meditate or pray: believe in God, the universe, energy, alignment, the cortex, vibration, frequency, gratitude, harmony, balance, positivity, the power of miracle, life is magic, angels, love, abundance, blessings, Lord, Holy Spirit, and Jesus.

For thirty days, practice gratitude, always being grateful on a daily basis. It will make you happier, and you will receive more blessings.

SOLUTION

When you surround yourself with positive people, the people who disagree with you will disappear. When you have a problem and are undecided on what to do, just lie back and let God do it for you. Place your mindset on the right and positive pathway.

The Meaning of Dreams

WHEN YOU SLEEP DEEPLY AND have a beautiful dream, you may want to interpret it. In one of my dreams, I was pregnant and gave birth to twins—a daughter and a son. I held my baby son and was happy, but I was looking for my baby girl. I ran to the nursery, and my mother came to me and said, "Don't worry. The baby is asleep in the crib." Then I ran to the crib and pulled away the blanket so I could see her face—and it was my face. The baby was me and smiled at me.

Here's my interpretation of this dream: The baby boy was my muscular side, and it shows that I am strong, independent, and free of anyone's control. On the other hand, I was looking for my baby girl and could not find her. My mother was there and gave me strength and power when she said there was no reason to worry. When I saw the baby in the crib, I found my feminine side, the part of me that was missing because I was looking for her. There is always harmony or balance in oneself.

Another dream related to a book of devotions for every day of year, *Jesus Calling*, by Sarah Young. A couple of days ago, the following brief verse became one of my favorites: "Wear me" is essentially thinking my own thoughts and clothing my mind in *me* for each day.

The night after I read this verse, I dreamed that Alison, former mother-in-law, invited me to a beautiful house and hired a tailor to make many dresses for me. I tried on all the new clothes and was happy to wear those dresses.

Then I said to Alison, "My plan is to remove the old clothes from my closet and replace them with all new ones."

The interpretation of this dream is that the new clothes indicate my new faith to become close to God. The new clothes, made by a tailor, means that God gave me faith. New clothes mean new protection. They were gifts from Alison because she is the one who always wanted me to be happy and successful.

Another dream was about Jesus. On October 19, 2016, the day of my graduation from master's program, I decided to give my heart to Jesus and was baptized in the private place. However, I'd never had a dream about Jesus until recently.

In the early morning, before sunrise, I was sleeping and dreamed that Jesus called my name. There was a very nice voice calling me: "Yeganeh."

And I responded, "Yes?" Then I woke myself up with my loud voice. It was a peaceful moment.

My interpretation of this dream: Jesus wanted me to be hopeful and grateful in this moment of my life. I am open to any culture and religion and feel united to different groups; I see them as a one. I respect any ethnicity. I believe people are people, whether they are white or black. We are all a gift from God. Our mission in this world is to help one another and learn to have goals and dreams in order to reach God and become morally perfect. By the way, the next day I purchased the book *Jesus Calling*.

During that time, I was working in home care. I had more dreams about my mother. It seems she is happy that I am taking take care of the elderly. Maybe I make her happy because I always treat my clients like I treated her. All these dreams of my mother inspired me to stop feeling guilty. In my dreams, my mother hugs me and kisses me, and she just stares at me. I hope she always has peace in her soul.

SOLUTION

When you have a nice dream, write it down on paper and then let your therapist interpret it for you. Sometimes, your dream is a part of your real goal and purpose in life.

$\mathscr{H}armony, Center, Balance$

A SIGNIFICANT WAY TO FIND your center and keep harmony in your life is advanced meditation. This technique should be practiced and followed precisely. Manifest into reality the way your life wants to be—love, joy, and peace. As you concentrate on the abundance in the world, not the wealth, you will see how to pay attention to the expansion of the universe. Then you can open your mind to understanding awareness and consciousness.

According to Max Plank (1948), when you close your eyes, your mind should think about the deep darkness of space. When you reach to the manifestation of the level of integrity, regularity, and unity, you may feel profoundly happy, as if you have everything. It would be a transcendent experience to feel happy without any reason. In reality, this type of feeling is very special, as the frequency of energy is released from the brain and flows to the heart, and people think they are connected to the initial source.

With meditation and correct breathing, you can open the chakras in your body to find the center and harmony. Then you can live with energy, love, joy, and peace. Chakra means *wheel* and refers to the energy points in your body. Exercising your chakras can result in controlling mood, temperature, and body health.

Controlling your chakras could directly influence your mental, physical, and spiritual health. You could improve your health and find a new, alternative way to see the world. If you want to have a clear mind and talk to God, pray, and then listen to him by meditating. I would love to meditate every day, specifically when I need to make a new decision.

The closer you are to God, the more likely you will be to find your creativity and talents. If you explore your hidden natural skills, you may be more fulfilled and will achieve your goals. Gradually, the power of this method informs you on what your mission is in life. Each talent will be added to your previous ideas; then, with your knowledge, you can develop a new aspect.

When you look at the history, you'll see that every generation notices how life has changed and improved, with new ideas and technologies. In reality, life goes on and is continued in the way it is. The good thing is that, as human beings, people are gifted and clever. Luckily, they always complete the past with hidden, natural talents in order to make the world an immortal place.

SOLUTION

By using mindfulness, you will increase your self-esteem and self-confidence. You will bring your life to the center of harmony and balance. Stay away from fear. You can do it; you're worth it. Follow your dream to reach your goal and achieve the career you want. Be strong; find a solution and change your mood with the tools of hope, happiness, and compassion. Just let it go and move on. Create some tasks to stay strong and be confident. You can do activities such as gardening, cooking, yoga, painting, or reading, to name a few.

What is a Chakra?

THE MAIN CHAKRA STARTS FROM the root of spinal cord. There are seven chakras, and their meanings are as follows:

CHAKRA LOCATED/ASSOCIATION/ELEMENT/COLOR

1. Base of spine/survival, security/earth/red (I understand)
2. Sacral abdominal/emotion, sexuality/water/orange (I see)
3. Solar plexus/self-esteem/fire/yellow (I talk)
4. Heart over the sternum/love, hope/air/green (I love)
5. Throat/throat communication/sound/blue (I do)
6. Third-eye, center of forehead/imagination/light/indigo (I feel)
7. Crown, top of the head/consciousness/thought/violet (I am)

All these chakras are responsible for linking with the physical and energy levels. Chakras' function is to bring energy into the nerves from the base to the top of the head. The transfer of the energy is from chakra number 1 to chakra number 7. When you breathe within these chakras, your life will be improved by changing your mood, emotions, and health.

Meditation and breathing from the chakras encourages you to respect your respiratory system, to give value to your breathing, and to readdress the way your body systems function.

The power of love allows you to take care of yourself. The body is like a safe place to stay in peace. The only thing you need to do is believe in yourself. Based on your beliefs, you will stay positive. Every one of your cells will stay healthy and young. Also, you will be happy without reason, and this can be a great strategy for reducing negativity.

There are many exercises for keeping you positive. For instance, every morning when you get up, show gratitude and pray to God to start a new day and a new beginning for you. Make a plan and promise yourself that you will have a good day.

Some projects are hard to do at first. However, pick the hardest one to finish first. You will have a great feeling after working hard. Then make great coffee or hot tea as a break. You are worth it, so have a little treat after you finish your projects. Life always is full of surprises. Have fun, and most of all, don't take life too seriously.

I believe life is like a theater scene; we have to play our own roles. You are responsible for presenting a great role in order to fit into society. Learn specific skills. I encourage you to grow and improve in the job you love.

Working at a profession you love helps you to enjoy every single day and to stay more focused, which will increase your creativity. Making something on your own can be a joyful work, and no matter how difficult it is, you will be proud of what you have accomplished in your life.

SOLUTION

Balancing your chakras help you to find your center. When you do this technique, your body starts to work with your mind at the same time. There is an awareness that works with your thoughts to keep your life in balance. The power of chakra practice, meditation, gratitude, and prayers will help you to stay away from negativity.

Meditation

SOMETIMES, YOU NEED TO SET boundaries with loved ones. Any person needs space during the day. If you are a mother, you need to get away for a short time to refresh yourself. I have found my favorite place in my home for meditation and to be on own. The exercise of intentional breathing makes you stronger and more fulfilled in challenging life.

First of all, do the easy breathing exercise. Just breathe normally for six seconds. Pause your breath for six seconds. Then breathe out for six seconds. Continue for two cycles. At the end, lie down on your stomach for ten minutes.

There is also a technique called *fingerhold practice* that combines breathing and holding each finger to manage emotions and stress.

Hold your thumb for forty-five seconds to help you not be upset. Then, hold your index finger to reduce fear and your middle finger to reduce anger. Hold your ring finger for forty-five seconds to prevent worry, and finally hold your little finger to decrease your bad feelings. When you are free, you can use this technique to balance your emotions on a daily basis. After you learn these different skills, your life will be changed profoundly to the next level.

SOLUTION

Your life will open to a new chapter with different aspects. Day by day, your perspective of your life will enter into the new phase. Based on my experiences, I have decided to divide my different affirmations to improve my awareness.

A Good Leader

AS A PERSON IN THIS universe, you have different traits and characteristics. It is your responsibility to recognize your abilities, talents, and skills. The unity of love, trust, and respect is the best method to connect with yourself and others. According to Jason Kiesau (2014), creating a culture of respect, love, trust, togetherness, and fun in the home can lead to closer families. Being a good leader depends on your relationship with your family.

The head of the family can be a female or a male; there is no gender differences in the twenty-first century. Being a leader in the family has many responsibilities. You may use the win-win technique, which is a handy and useful solution for every dilemma you have. Moreover, you will create peace and love between two parties. There is no reason that one could lose. Both people are happy for the new decisions that are made. Unfortunately, this technique does not work in a capitalistic society. Most business relationships resemble a seesaw on the playground.

Based on the study of Jason Kiesau, a person is a good leader based on three things: vision, action, and spirit. Whatever you do, based on the commitment you have toward your family, you are responsible for taking the right action. Then you should do it with a spirit that inspires others to be and do their best.

Every family has value. As a leader, you may share what you respect and what is of value to you. We are unique and deserve the best in this world. We have a choice to be happy. Therefore, family first. Teach your family that the relationship you have is based on love, fairness, security, and safety. When your children are raised in this pleasant environment, they will learn how to make important decisions on their own. They will recognize their weak and strong points while they seek their goals, careers, schools, and relationships. After all, when the children are on the appropriate pathway, they will enjoy an amazing life that was addressed by the leadership of their parents or guardians.

A good leader represents the right thing to the members of the family. Value your time. When you are on the treadmill, read a book; when you are in the kitchen and waiting for your coffee to get warm, do a couple of minutes of exercise.

Always focus every second of your effort, and do everything by multitasking. You will feel that you are living in the moment, and you will be active, emotionally, physically, and mentally.

Be open to the different cultures. Having self-respect and self-value allows you to give your family the choice to evaluate other cultures and realize that people are respectful and have their own values as well.

SOLUTION

Recognize your weak points and strong points. Initially, when you are angry at yourself, just look for the reason for the dilemma and what you can do to make yourself calm and happy again.

For instance, when you wake up in the morning, if you are not feeling good, just check your thoughts and remember the reason for this struggle. When you understand the reason for your sadness, you can be open to your problem, shift it to the good feelings, and change it quickly. Remember that life is beautiful, and we can remain in this beautiful life.

Keep Your Boundaries

WE SHOULD LEARN HOW TO keep our boundaries with others. It is a good exercise for everyone. Children can learn not to cross a line and to keep their distance from the people who want to be alone. Following the rules can start in a small group, like a family. Keep your promises to everyone who trusts you. Children count on you. For instance, spending quality time with each other encourages you to feel closer and to feel great about your family.

As a result, your children will remember you with love and respect. Life is a learning process. Playing games and doing different activities together, like biking, fishing, crafts, and sports, can help children use their creativity and talents.

You do not need others' approval. Always be yourself; enjoy and trust life. The way you carry yourself can show that you are comfortable in your own skin.

There is a principle and discipline for parents to raise their children. Therefore, when you respect your family, the children can learn how to react nicely. In fact, you will teach your loved ones how to treat you. In addition, the acceptance step would be the alternative way to cope and deal with any problems you have in real life. When you reach this step, you definitely have respect for people's boundaries.

Respect yourself and others. Don't ask too many questions of others. You are not in this life to control other or to be curious about people's lives. Keep your boundaries and privacy. People get tired if you ask questions all the time. Practice the silent treatment, and let people talk to you and tell their own stories. You can just listen to them and wait for them to express their pain and feelings. They need you to listen to them. Then, they will be ready to pay attention to you and whatever you want to say.

SOLUTION

Always remember that you teach people how to treat you. If you respect people and talk nicely, you will say to them, "Treat me with respect." Keep your privacy and boundaries to live in peace. This is a great practice to follow with your children. You can have a close relationship with them without being controlling. Let them live and experience life by themselves, Let them follow their own dreams. Let them become heroes in their own stories.

Healthy Relationship

SURROUND YOURSELF WITH POSITIVE PEOPLE. If you change your thoughts with positivity, you will attract the same thing. You can find a great date if you stop thinking of the previous relationship. It will be easier if you change your old patterns, and open a new chapter of your life. Take it easy, and stop blaming yourself. The past is past. Move on and forget about the negative aspects of your memories.

I have blocked certain memories; I have trained my brain to erase all the nonsense and pathetic thoughts from my consciousness. With meditation, I can provide positive strength and power to my consciousness in order to clear my mind and to obtain amazing knowledge. This will enable me to feel good about myself.

My consciousness is God, Holy Spirit, and Jesus. With this belief, I am sober-minded. There is an exercise that you can do it throughout the day.

Be a faithful to your consciousness. When you want to fix or do something for others, do your best, from the bottom of your heart. Be fair, and enjoy your time when you want to commit your promise to people.

This powerful practice allows you to be open to the world of abundance. It is one of my favorite techniques for sticking on this pathway. Pay it forward. You are capable of unconditional love. The first step is to learn to love yourself. Then, you are able to accept yourself and others in the way they are. Next, respect your own and others' boundaries. For instance, sometimes parents have to treat their children roughly. They love them, but for their children's sake, they might react harshly.

For example, parents unconditionally love their children, but sometimes they have to be stern when they want their lives to get back to normal. The power of love upholds the family and helps it to become safe and confident. Life is a learning process; we have the choices to learn from our loved ones and to give them unconditional love.

STOP CONTROLLING

If someone asks for advice, you can talk to that person and follow up with him or her. You are not here in this world to change people or to fix others' problems. Ask your friends in a support group to think of you if you want to help people as a volunteer.

Stop being controlling in your relationships. Emphasize this phrase: *it's none of your business.* Let people live. If they need help, they are free to ask you. Otherwise, it does not make any sense to resolve their problems without their permission.

Let your loved ones experience their own lives. They are free to make their own decisions. They have choices and can see the right things to do. If they depend on you, their lives might depend on you. They might be burned out and unable to use their creativity to make their choices.

Forgiveness is important in a healthy relationship. First of all, forgive yourself; then forgive others and move on from the past. If you don't remove the resentment from your mind, you will stress out from making immoral judgments.

On the other hand, when you forgive and forget, you will be free of hidden painful memories.

Gradually, your life will change to address the right pattern, and you might invite positive and caring people into your life.

If you miss having a healthy relationship, you might like to start with working on yourself. Decide what you really want from your loved one.

1. Make a long list, and write every detail you feel you need.
2. Believe in yourself; you deserve more.
3. Explore your weakest point.
4. When you love yourself, you will raise your self-esteem and self-confidence.
5. Do you need someone to make you complete and happier?
6. What is your goal?
7. What is your interest? You can focus on just on your interest.
8. Find your talents and skills. Grow only in your talents.

SOLUTION

If you want to have a healthy relationship with a loved one, meditate every night for forty days. In deep meditation, you will see your soul mate. You can talk to him or her. Try to use your imagination.

Living in the Present Time

WHEN YOU GO FOR A walk, focus your attention on nature. Take the deep breath in the morning breeze, and smell the roses and jasmine all over the area. If you are happy and focus on your steps, you will hear the birds singing delightfully.

Other people may pass by and say hello to you. Be happy for all the beauty in nature. The power of gratitude can tell you that the universe has a wonderful order and arrangement for any creatures.

Living in the moment can teach you how to be a patient and wait for the big harvest in autumn. When farmers plant seeds, they will take care of the fields, watering them and planting in the correct location. Then, if they do that, they will reap a harvest at the right time.

Be patient while waiting and look for everything in time. Living in the present time makes you to raise your focus and attention as well. Yesterday is the past and a memory. You can't predict the future. You can make a plan for your life, but there's no guarantee it will follow your same plan.

Stop ruining your present time by worrying over the past and future. The smart person is the one who learns from experiences and skills from the past and uses those tools to make an amazing future. With prayer and meditation, you can clear your mind from negativity. The learning process makes you increase your awareness to develop the new things.

Keep following this practice. Focus on the present time, and you will see what is going on around you. In general, you can see and hear precisely what is around you. For instance, when you are driving, look at the people on the street—what are they doing? How many black cars or red cars are behind you or in front of your car? Pay more attention to the present time. You can create more games to stay focused on what you do during the time you are awake. Then you enter into an abundance of time. When you think this way, you will have plenty of time to do so many things without getting stressed.

It means you have entered into the prosperity of time. In such a world, when you live sixty seconds, it passes like sixty minutes. The time becomes limitless, and you have plenty of time to follow your dreams and talents.

SOLUTION

Keep changing and learning new practices regarding the appreciation of the present time. Value your time, and bring your attention to the present time by taking deep breaths to observe and watch the beauty of life.

Do not run away from the present time; just stay there and stop thinking about the past and the future. By breathing several times and concentrating on the way you are breathing, you will learn how to stay focused and will appreciate everything you have in your life.

High Frequency of Vibration Manifestation

NEGATIVE THOUGHTS VS. POSITIVE THOUGHTS

Negative thoughts: I am not good enough. I do not deserve it. I feel I am behind.

Negative feelings: fears, disappointment, shame.

Negative behaviors: Looking for approval. I don't give myself a chance. I am not good enough.

Schema: behavior, feeling, action.

Schemer: When I can't succeed, what should I do not to fail?

SOLUTION

Pray, and ask God to help you. Practice gratitude, mediation, and exercise. Surround yourself with positive people. Focus on self-care, healthy food, going to therapy or group therapy, working with the children or the elderly, increasing your self-esteem and self-confidence, and believing in yourself.

Negativity is highly powerful. Your negative energy and the way you focus on the issue can be related to stopping the frequency of the positives. You don't want bad things happen to you, but when you keep concentrating on your negative unwanted things, the negative thoughts are attracted to you right away.

Positive thoughts: positive experiences, positive behavior, positive action. I want to take care of myself. I am happy and feeling great.

Positive experiences: The power of gratitude allows me to see the miracles in my life. When I go to bed, I will count the number of positive events in my day. When I am happy and hopeful, everything turns into a simple and joyful time. With positivity you can love yourself and appreciate of every cell of your body.

If you want to become forever young, show appreciation of every single molecule in your body. In addition, give your love to every object you touch or own. The power of gratitude is one of the things in your heart's "Holy Spirit" that provides everything for you just ask for it. When you have a closer relationship to Spirit, your value is changed, and you feel joy and peace for everyone in your heart.

You can start to believe and trust yourself to do something right. When you are on this journey, the possibility of success will be priceless. Before you know it, life will become magical for you.

What is the frequency of vibration that is manifesting, and how you can apply to yourself?

Can it be about working hard for what you want to be in the future? The more you understand about your awareness, the more you can release a naturally higher vibration. Just allow the vibration to flow in and out. The energy of vibration will be around you and will turn your life toward an easier process. The naturally high frequency of vibration means awareness and is a receptor of the reality of who you are. Let it go to the power of vibration, and choose what you want to be.

The Unity and Unification of the World

MY MISSION IN THIS UNIVERSE is to spread love and unity and to purify your heart. I am in love with myself and see people as one. This affirmation can describe the meaning of unity. I respect to different cultures and religions. I believe that every one of us has a hidden talent when we are born. We can explore our talents and realize that our mission can reveal our talents to the world.

We are here to complete each other by offering additional knowledge and information to modify any point, such as with inventions, discoveries, science, and philosophy. I want inner peace for the universe. My dream is to reach God with love and unity. One of my biggest dreams is to remove the borders from the different lands so there will not be any nationalities, and people could say they are from the earth.

Unfortunately, the name of God and religions in some countries and governments would be involved in crimes and unjust movements and would receive irrational achievements.

There is no war in my ideal place. People smile and greet one another. There is no pain, no problems; people care about each other. There is no discrimination, no color, and no race. There are no exclusive religions and no judgmental people. We are a masterpiece of God.

Another word—we are Muslim, Christian, Jewish, Buddhist, etc. God wants us to become united by love and peace.

SOLUTION

Self-love, responsibility, seeking for a solution instead of a problem, acceptance, gratitude, prayers, meditation, exercises, traveling, God's grace, and helping people—God always gives me grace to become a better person. Do not take life too seriously because life changes all the time. Learn how to trust people. Life is all about the learning process. While serving people, promote yourself to be sure and secure.

When you believe in yourself, it's a blessing. You get your faith from God.

Life is Always Beautiful

AFTER MY DIVORCE, I FELT relieved that I had made a good decision. I was alone; none of my family was here. I knew I should move on and make myself calm down. On the last day of my marriage, I woke up sad and could not stand to stay in the relationship. I asked God to show me a sign and a miracle. After I prayed, everything turned out better than I'd expected.

I looked in the mirror and told myself, "Your sons have gone to college. They are safe and happy. There is nothing left here for you." I closed my eyes to think about my sons and realized how much I loved them. I wanted to bring peace, love, and comfort to them under the same roof—just me and my sons, as a respectable and caring family. My sons should learn how to treat a woman like a lady.

I wanted my sons to see the truth and respect others, especially women, in a great manner. Suddenly, a voice in my head told me, *Go! What are you waiting for?* After a couple of months, I left home.

I was blessed and started to do the gratitude practice. I kept repeating the thanksgiving until I became a master of this practice. It was a great experience to have the mind and body working together. Once the body started to believe, the mind received the emotional sign. Then, I could feel the appreciation of gratitude in my heart.

I opened my heart and believed I could make my life in a marvelous way. I purchased my lovely home. My sons were excited to live together again, with peace and love and having amazing experiences in the same place called a cozy home.

I was reborn and wanted to breathe and start a new life. I knew that some miracle would happen. In my heart, I found love and compassion. I realized that I needed to follow a principle to rebuild the beautiful life that I deserved. First of all, I forgave myself and others. It was a difficult process, but I did that for my own sake, to receive peace and compassion. I completely modified everything so that I could see the reality and be more honest with myself.

I had to understand what my purpose of living is and why I am here. How could I gain information to help and support myself and others? The family has value, and we respect the way we are. I started to read and follow many spiritual practices of gratitude.

I purchased the house, and my sons and I lived together for years. As a family, we had a wonderful time together.

Healthy life: Every morning when I wake up, I pray, meditate, and read *Jesus Calling* to get more energy for the rest of day. I have a glass of warm water with a couple of drops of lemon juice and get ready for a thirty-minute walk. Then, I bathe and have a breakfast of eggs, cheese, walnuts, almonds, honey, a piece of bread, and a cup of hot tea. My day is started at 10:00 a.m. If I decide to stay home, I cook and garden. All these chores keep me happy, and I see the love and great energy around my home. By practicing gratitude, I open my heart to feel joy and happiness in my life.

When I get back from work at 3:00 p.m., I try to have lunch with my two roommates; they are like my family. We like to support each other, and we care about what we need in our lives. I am so blessed to have them as close friends and a new family. After lunch, we clean up the kitchen together, and everyone likes to go back to their rooms and rest and also do their own business.

This is a good opportunity for me to write, read, and listen to jazz piano. After 7:00 p.m., we have a meeting in my living room for tea time and having healthy snacks. Sometimes when we are together, we like to go for a walk or meditate to maintain the positive energy and naturally high vibrations. Before we go to bed, we eat a small portion of healthy food to sleep well.

I have been highly blessed with what I have in my life. I love my roommates; they are my new family. In addition, my house has been a great place for my international students. They are always grateful for the welcoming and warm hospitality. Most of them are attorneys and businesspeople in their own countries. Everything I have now is because of my belief system. Sometimes, I am really pleased and happy, as if God is living in my home.

When you have a plan and you are willing to continue this plan, don't share it with people who are pessimistic, hopeless, and living in fear. Such people have trust issues and can't trust others. Specifically, they always disagree with the people who want to grow and change their lives and open their lives to new ideas. Mostly, they think the advertisements of some new product is expensive and fake. They become very nervous when they see you are willing to buy that new products, and they try to make you anxious and fragile. The interesting thing is that when the seller tries to give them a discount or offers it at no cost, they say, "No, there must be something wrong with this product if you're giving it away." They always say no about anything. Most of the time, even if they agree with your opinion, they will start their conversations with *no.*

Overall, the people who think like that take life too seriously. They are not happy in their lives at all. Mostly, they think that to have the simple life, you need to work hard and always be under pressure. They think that if you are a positive person, you will drown in your dream, and you will never get back to reality—but life is not designed like that.

Life is beautiful. We have to have a dream. If you have a new idea in mind, you may visualize and imagine that your dream comes true. You will be happy, and it will bring a smile to your face—and if so, why not?

There are so many techniques you can practice to receive your goals. According to Dr. Wayne Dyer, "Visualizing can help your dreams come true." Therefore, when you repeat your imagined scene, your subconscious mind is further impressed, information becomes available, and circumstances are created, all in favor of that goal. For example, a woman may receive a surprise phone call from an old friend who recently moved near her. Her brain gets ready to filter her imagination.

The moment you decided to talk about your goal, all the vehicles are provided for you to receive the thing you want. For instance, one of my friends wanted to learn French. As soon as she decided to learn this language, her brain started to filter and collect all the information about the people, language, and culture in France. She also met someone to teach her French.

It means everything—you just ask the universe to give it to you.

SOLUTION

The power of gratitude can works in the same way—the more you are grateful, the more things you will receive. Every night, when I go to bed, I say, "Thank you, thank you, and thank you for everything you have done for me during the day."

Family Value

WHEN I WAS A LITTLE girl, my mother was a great storyteller. I was inspired by one of her stories. It was about an old lady who lived by herself. She was very caring and kind, and one rainy day, she decided to open her house to let in the different animals who were tired and restless from the storm. They had a good time together and decided to stay there with the old lady. And they lived happily ever after.

I always loved stories with great endings, like *Cinderella*—the little girl who never gave up and made a beautiful fantasy world for herself with a bunch of the mice in the house. Her world was simple enough; she understood and recognized the beauty, goodness, and high quality of being a kind person. In the world of Cinderella, there were no bad people. Everyone helped and cared about each other. They were happy and got together to celebrate everything. Cinderella had been raised well with her parents, but after a while, her life became complicated. Still, she was strong and always hopeful that her life could be changed. She also believed that her life situation, whatever it was, would not stay the same.

Sometimes, life is complicated, but never lose hope. There always are good possibilities in your life.

As a result of those stories, my life was inspired by different characters to change my everyday life. After my divorce, everything was planned for what to do with my life. The power of gratitude told me what my goal was in this universe. I met so many good people in my life. I always showed my appreciation to them because without them, it would have been impossible to start on my journey. I finished my school with a bachelor's degree in psychology and found a job for seven years as a preschool teacher.

Working with children of different ages was a good experience for me, since it encouraged me to stay calm and forget about my past. After getting my master's degree, I was ready to change my job and become a social worker. Working with substance-abuse clients for three years taught me to empower my lifestyle and realize who I am and what I want from my life.

I always wanted to become a family therapist and help people. When you have a goal, everything goes smoothly, and you can enjoy your life. You can get help from prayers and meditation, which will make you calm and relaxed when you want to make a final decision on small and big goals; you can even use it on a daily basis.

When you go to bed, go over your schedule for the next day. Ask yourself what important plan you should do on a daily basis. Always do the hardest project first, in early morning, when you are off and staying home. This technique will bring your satisfaction in your life, and you will be content to keep doing the rest of your work. When you do your jobs, set your timer to see how can you finish them without pushing yourself.

It means you value your time and the job you are doing. Don't make yourself bored; there are always things to do around the house. After you finish, you can give yourself a reward, such as taking a break with a cup of tea or coffee and sitting down in your favorite chair while you listen to music.

It is very important to care about yourself and love yourself. I believe that love is the approbation of the world. Love brings inner peace, compassion, and the power of abundance. Every night, when you want to close the chapter for your day, do self-hygiene. Sometimes, I cannot sleep right away; it takes time. I use oil or lotion to massage my feet while I close my eyes for two minutes. Sometimes I add one teaspoon of magnesium powder to a cup of hot water and drink it. Then I sleep like a baby.

Some single people over fifty years old seem intent on being alone in their lives. They got used to this type of lifestyle, and they are not able to trust people. The good news is that when they start loving and taking care of themselves, the power of gratitude slowly can allow them to become loveable persons who are concerned about the people who live around them. Then, they will be capable of being loved and loving someone.

When you are optimistic and open to different aspects, then you will be able to meet the positive people who make you happy and understand your every move. We tell each other that we have chemistry or that we click with each other because of the natural frequency of vibrations.

Certainly, when you have this new attitude, you will find a loved one who has a great spirit—someone who will support you like a best buddy, make you laugh, and live with you for better or worse, for richer or poorer; someone who will love and care about you; the one who will stand by your side to catch you before you fall.

I love my new family and am proud of myself and my friends. In 2016, I was broke and a little bit upset, but I knew that God, Holy Spirit, and Jesus were always in my heart. My house has a great energy, and everyone who lives there is affected by those energies, helping them to be healthy and happy. That is what they've said, and my friends always emphasize this point.

There was a day when I ran out of money but wanted to pay the bill for my homeowners' association (HOA). Unfortunately, I didn't have enough to pay the bill. I went to talk to a reliable lady called Lucy, who lived in my neighborhood. She also was a member of the HOA board. I told her my story and asked if I could pay in installments until my balance was zero.

She said, "Let me think about it; no worries."

I came back home and kept praying for my problems to be solved soon. Lucy tried to find a job for me to make money so I could take care of this bill.

At nine o'clock the same night, she knocked on my door. She smiled and said, "Your problem is solved, Yeganeh!"

I looked at her. "How?"

"One of our neighbors has a heart problem, and she is looking for a good person to sleep at her house at night. I think you are a good candidate to give her comfort so she wouldn't be alone every night."

I wasn't sure about doing this every night. If I went there, what about my room? I love to sleep in my bed and be comfortable. I asked God to please help me to know what to do. The next day, Lucy took me to meet and have an interview with the neighbor.

When Lucy told me her name, I said, "This neighbor is my friend. She is still young and heathy and does not need anyone to take care of her."

When we knocked on her door, my dear friend Hamideh opened the door and hugged me, saying, "Yeganeh, you are just like my daughter. I've known you for such a long time. Why didn't you tell me that you needed help? Don't you understand that's what friends are for? I want you to come here at night. One of my rooms would belong to you. Bring your stuff to your room. I will pay you enough money to take care of your bills as well."

I was so happy, it was as if the world belongs to me. I felt like I was the wealthiest woman in the world. A miracle happened to me on that unforgettable night. My beloved Hamideh allowed me to live with her as long as I wanted.

The next day, I got another roommate; she was one of my friends, and I rented my own room to her. She was added to my new family too. As a result, I was ready to take care of everything at home. Every day, I worked and help my client Connie. Then, I came back home and went to another job for three hours. Then at 6:00 p.m., I finished my job by bringing two kids from different schools to their house, helped them with their homework, and gave them dinner. Then I helped them take a bath and get ready for bed.

When their mother returned, I was relieved to get back to my home. I stayed in my home for a while, resting and chitchatting with my family, laughing, and having fun. At 10:00 p.m., I was ready to meet my beloved friend Hamideh. Every night, we had fun watching her favorite TV shows together, and at midnight, I would go to my room and study for my exam.

Over the weekend, we got together either in my house or Hamideh's house to make meals and have fun. We laughed and amused one another as a caring family.

Unfortunately, Covid-19 took us in a different direction. We now are staying home and are not able to meet each other as we had been doing.

I learned so many things from Hamideh. She is one of the most important women in my life. The relationship I have with her is like a mother and a daughter. It is more than friendship. She is part of my family.

SOLUTION

This is a very important point of view: when someone takes a step to do something for you, always appreciate his or her love and kindness. This is a beautiful lesson and experience, and you may learn how to pay it forward.

My mother always told me, "Be proud of what you have, and work hard to become independent. Help people, no matter what. Love is recycled—you get what you give."

Trustee, Forbidden, Legitimate

ANY RELIGION, PHILOSOPHY, OR MYSTICISM belief says to love others as you love yourself. Respect others' rights as you take care of yours. These ideas and beliefs depend on the way people are raised. *Trustee* is noun that means you are responsible for holding or maintaining someone's property, money, or other things.

The person who is a trustee is humble and respectful and understands the problem. No matter what, the trustee is always there for you. These people respect your privacy and tend to respect boundaries. A trustee is ready to hear your repetitive stories again. He or she knows forbidden and legitimate things.

This person asks for your permission before getting any small thing from your house or office. Trustees are secure and reliable. Trustees live in the abundance of health, love, and wealth.

Because they are always happy for everything, they have happiness, and the universe will provide whatever they want. They love and help others to stand on their own feet. They believe in this belief system. It is not very important for them to become a hero of the people's stories. They can control their own egos. As a result, it's worth it to do anything for them when they ask for help.

SOLUTION

This is my opinion, but I hope you agree with me: love yourself, be honest, be positive, believe in yourself, exercise, and treat others as you want to be treated. If you are happy or upset, visit the nursing home or a cemetery. Appreciate nature while you are walking. The power of gratitude is very important.

If you are tired of going to the grocery store, you could make it fun for yourself. Set up the time and make a list of what you need to buy. Put away a certain amount of money for the grocery. When you touch the fruits or any produce, just think about their taste and freshness. You can appreciate nature and the people who work so hard to bring the great quality of their products into the store for your tastes and satisfaction.

Printed in the United States
by Baker & Taylor Publisher Services